Pebble® Plus

Investigate the Seasons

Let's Look at Fall

Revised Edition

by Sarah L. Schuette

CAPSTONE PRESS
a capstone imprint

Pebble Plus is published by Capstone Press,
1710 Roe Crest Drive, North Mankato, Minnesota 56003
www.capstonepub.com

Library of Congress Cataloging-in-Publication Data
is available on the Library of Congress website.

ISBN 978-1-5435-0860-4 (library binding)
ISBN 978-1-5435-0876-5 (paperback)
ISBN 978-1-5435-0880-2 (ebook pdf)

Editorial Credits
Sarah Bennett, designer; Tracy Cummins, media researcher,
Laura Manthe, production specialist

Photo Credits
Shutterstock: Dave Allen Photography, 7, DmZ, 5, Erik Mandre,
15, FotoRequest, 13, Grisha Bruev, 9, images72, 17, Liubou
Yasiukovich, Cover Design Element, Manamana, 11, Nancy Gill,
19, nikitsin.smugmug.com, 1, Piotr Krzeslak, Cover, Sofiaworld,
3, Victor Grow, 21

Note to Parents and Teachers

The Investigate the Seasons set supports national science
standards related to weather and life science. This book
describes and illustrates the season of fall. The images support
early readers in understanding the text. The repetition of words
and phrases helps early readers learn new words. This book also
introduces early readers to subject-specific vocabulary words,
which are defined in the Glossary section. Early readers may
need assistance to read some words and to use the Table of
Contents, Glossary, Read More, Internet Sites, Critical Thinking
Questions, and Index sections of the book.

Printed in the United States   5743

Pebble Plus is published by Capstone Press,
1710 Roe Crest Drive,
North Mankato, Minnesota 56003
www.capstonepub.com

Library of Congress Cataloging-in-Publication Data
Names: Hall, Margaret, 1947- , author.
Title: Penguins and their chicks : a 4D book / by
Margaret Hall.
Description: Revised edition.. | North Mankato,
Minnesota : Capstone Press, 2018. | Series: Pebble plus.
Animal offspring | Includes bibliographical references
and index. | Audience: Ages 4 to 8.
Identifiers: LCCN 2017037873 (print) | LCCN 2017054337
(ebook) | ISBN 9781543508659 (eBook PDF) | ISBN
9781543508253 (hardcover) | ISBN 9781543508376 (pbk.)
Subjects: LCSH: Penguins—Infancy—Juvenile literature.
| Parental behavior in animals—Juvenile literature.
Classification: LCC QL696.S473 (ebook) | LCC QL696.
S473 H35 2018 (print) | DDC 598.4713/92—dc23
LC record available at https://lccn.loc.gov/2017037873

Editorial Credits
Gina Kammer, editor; Sarah Bennett, designer; Morgan
Walters, media researcher;
Katy LaVigne, production specialist

Photo Credits
Shutterstock: Alexey Seafarer, 5, BMJ, left 21, Brandon
B, 9, ChameleonsEye, 19, jo Crebbin, 7, niall dunne,
15, Roger Clark ARPS, Cover, 3, left 20, right 20,
StanislavBeloglazov, 11, vladsilver, 17, right 21,
Volodymyr Goinyk, 13

Note to Parents and Teachers

The Animal Offspring set supports national science
standards related to life sciences. This book describes
and illustrates penguins and their chicks. The images
support early readers in understanding the text.
The repetition of words and phrases helps early readers
learn new words. This book also introduces early
readers to subject-specific vocabulary words, which are
defined in the Glossary section. Early readers may need
assistance to read some words and to use the Table of
Contents, Glossary, Read More, Internet Sites, Critical
Thinking Questions, and Index sections of the book.

Printed in the United States   5787

Table of Contents

It's Fall!

How do you know it's fall?

A cool breeze blows.

The weather is colder.

4

Leaves change color.

They flutter to the ground.

The sun sets earlier.
Fall days are shorter
than summer days.

9

Animals in Fall

What do animals do in fall?

Squirrels rush around.

They gather nuts

to store for winter.

Birds fly south.

They look

for warmer weather.

13

Bears search for a place

to hibernate.

Their fur coats grow thicker.

Plants in Fall

What happens

to plants in fall?

Ripe apples fill the orchard.

They're ready to be picked.

Corn ripens in the field.

It's ready to be harvested.

What's Next?

The temperature grows cold.

Fall is over.

What season is next?

Glossary

breeze—a gentle wind

flutter—to wave, flap, or float in a breeze; leaves flutter as they drop off tree branches

harvest—to gather crops that are ready to be picked; fall is a time for harvesting crops such as corn, soybeans, wheat, and oats

hibernate—to spend the winter in a deep sleep

orchard—a field or farm where fruit trees grow

ripen—to become ready to be picked

season—one of the four parts of the year; winter, spring, summer, and fall are seasons

weather—the condition outdoors at a certain time and place; weather changes with each season

Read More

Appleby, Alex. *What Happens in Fall?* Four Super Seasons. New York: Gareth Stevens Pub., 2014.

Brennan, Linda Crotta. *Leaves Change Color.* Tell Me Why. Ann Arbor, Mich.: Cherry Lake Publishing, 2015.

Herrington, Lisa M. *How Do You Know it's Fall?* Rookie Read-About Science. New York: Children's Press, 2014.

Internet Sites

Use FactHound to find Internet sites related to this book.

Visit *www.facthound.com*

Just type 9781543508604 and go.

Check out projects, games and lots more at
www.capstonekids.com

Critical Thinking Questions

1. Describe two signs that it is fall.

2. What do squirrels do in fall?

3. Describe what "harvest" means. Use the glossary to help you.

Index